Camels

by Sara Karnoscak

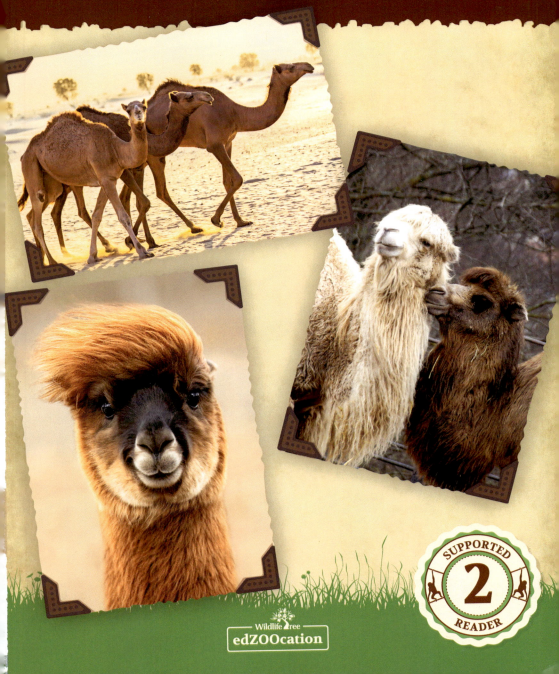

SUPPORTED
2
READER

Wildlife Tree
edZOOcation

Dedication:

For London, my adventurer.

–S.K.

For Leo, because camels are cool and so are you.

–T.S.

Author: Sara Karnoscak

Designer: Tiffany Swicegood

Editor: Tess Riley

With special thanks to Meri Lawrence, zookeeper, for her expert review of this book.

Photo Credits:

AdobeStock.com

Pixabay.com

Pexels.com

ISBN: 979-8-9859544-3-2

This book meets **Common Core** and **Next Generation Science** Standards.

Table of Contents

A Camel's Body

Two rows of extra-long eyelashes to keep out sand.

Nostrils that close to keep out sand.

Split upper lip with sides that move separately.

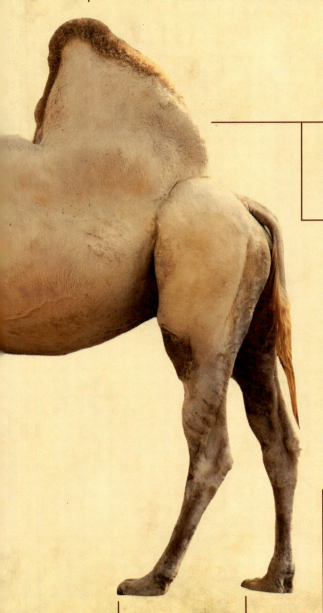

One or two humps
to store fat.

Wooly coat to
protect the body
from heat and cold.

Two toes on each
foot that help them
walk on the sand.

What's in a Hump?

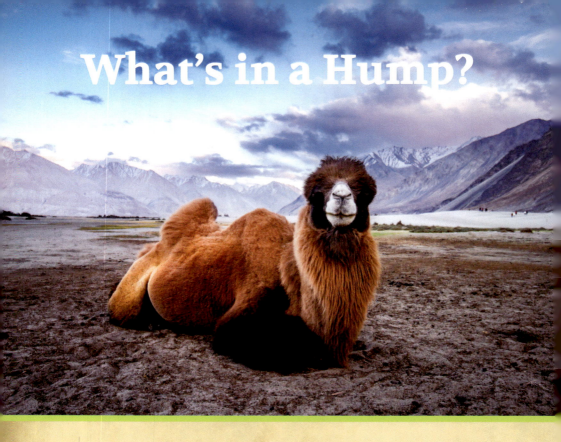

A camel's humps aren't filled with water. They're filled with fat! Camels can use the fat for food and water.

Camels do store water in their bodies, though. They store water in their blood. They store water in sacs in their stomachs.

When it's very hot, they can go four to seven days without water.

If there's food around with **moisture** in it, camels can go up to 10 months without drinking!

Moisture: *A small amount of water or other liquid.*

To help save water, they hardly **sweat**. They don't start to sweat until their body is 106 °F.

Sweat: *Moisture leaving your body through your skin.*

Tiptoeing Around

Can you tell which print is from a Camel?

If you guessed 8, you were right! Many pack animals have hooves. Camels don't, though. They have two toes on each foot. The toes spread when they walk. This makes it easier to walk on sand.

Native Australians used to think camel tracks were bum prints. They thought little spirits were sitting across the desert.

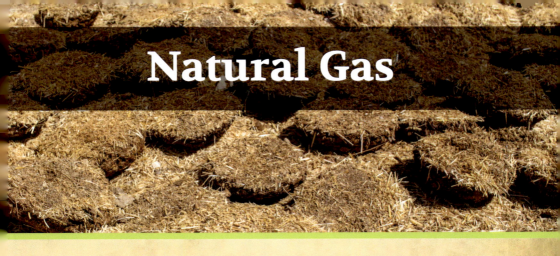

Natural Gas

All animals pass gas. But camels pass fuel! In some places, camel poop is burned for fuel.

Camels keep most of their moisture in their bodies. This makes their poop very dry. Perfect for burning!

Have you ever heard that camels spit? When they get scared, they bring up what's in their stomach and mix it with spit. Then – surprise! – they spit at what's scaring them.

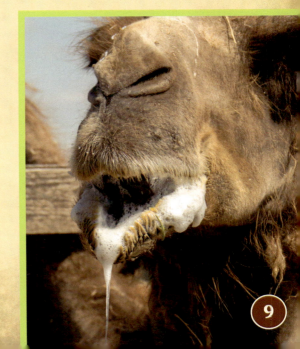

The Camel Family

There are three types of camel.

Dromedary

Bactrian

Wild Bactrian

Lamoids

Lamoids are part of the camel family, too.

Llamas are lamoids.

Alpacas are lamoids.

Vicuñas are lamoids.

Guanacos are lamoids.

How Many Humps?

How do you tell them apart?

Dromedaries have one hump. Like a letter D!

Bactrians have two humps. Like a letter B!

Lamoids have no hump.

Spot the Difference

Can you spot five differences in the pictures below?

Mommy and Me

When a camel is about to have her baby, she moves away from the herd. The new baby can walk with his mom 30 minutes after he's born. But they won't join the herd for about two more weeks.

Mom and baby will stay close for the next five years. She will teach him how to find food.

She will also teach him how to get along with the other camels.

Alpha Male: *The top male in a group.*

All the baby camels in the herd share a dad. There is only one **alpha male** in the herd.

What Does the Camel Say?

A lot! Camels moan… **bellow**… roar… and hum.

Bellow: *A roaring shout.*

Desert Travelers

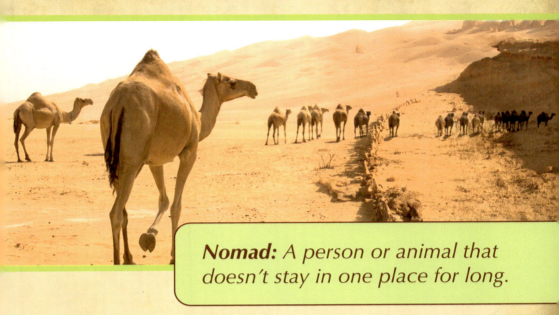

Nomad: *A person or animal that doesn't stay in one place for long.*

Camels are **nomads**. They travel around looking for food and water. They travel in groups called **caravans**.

Caravan: *A herd of camels.*

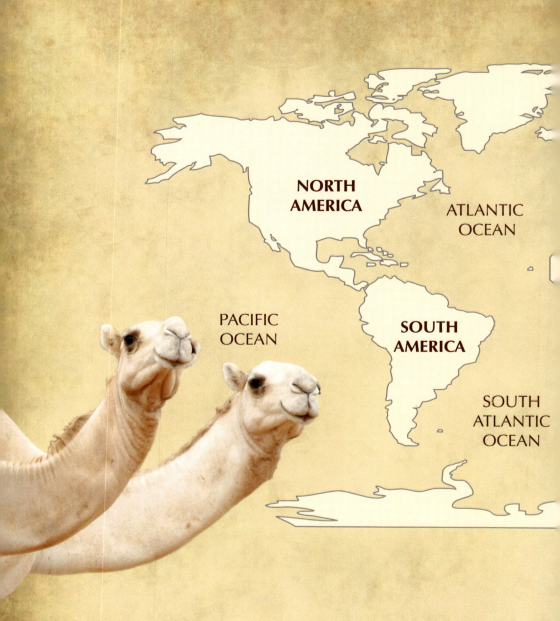

NORTH
AMERICA

ATLANTIC
OCEAN

PACIFIC
OCEAN

SOUTH
AMERICA

SOUTH
ATLANTIC
OCEAN

Different Camels Live in Different Places

ARCTIC OCEAN

RUSSIA

EUROPE

ASIA

PACIFIC
OCEAN

AFRICA

INDIAN
OCEAN

AUSTRALIA

ANTARCTICA

Wild camels live in Asia.

Domestic camels live in North Africa and the Middle East.

Feral camels live in Australia.

Domestic: *Tame. Not wild.*

Feral: *Gone wild after being tame.*

Camel Code

Use the key to decode the message.

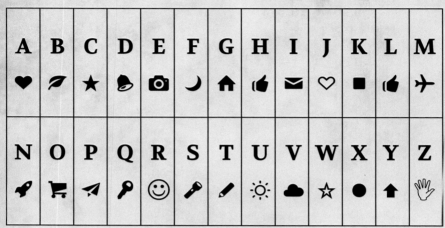

A	B	C	D	E	F	G	H	I	J	K	L	M
♥	🍃	★	🎩	📷	🌙	🏠	👍	✉	♡	■	👍	✈

N	O	P	Q	R	S	T	U	V	W	X	Y	Z
🚀	🛒	✈	🔑	☺	🔦	✏	☀	☁	☆	●	⬆	✋

Answer: THIRSTY AS A CAMEL.

Can you make your own
hidden message?

_____

_____

Goodnight Camel

Graze: *Eat grass.*

Camels are **diurnal**. They travel and **graze** during the day.

Diurnal: *Active during the day.*

They sleep at night.

Poking Around...

Camels are usually **herbivores**. They like to eat plants. But it can be hard to find food in the desert. So camels eat what they can find. Camels may eat….

CACTUS

FISH BONES

TRASH

TOXIC PLANTS

Herbivore: An animal that eats plants.

for Food

Camels have a special lip to help them. Their top lip is split. They can use their split lip to grab food that's hard to get. Just like you use your fingers!

A Day in the Life...

The camel wakes up early in the morning. He's hungry.

He joins the herd as they graze.

They're having cactus for breakfast. He uses his floppy lips to grab the cactus carefully.

# of a Camel

Then the herd travels to find more food. The sun is hot, but he doesn't break a sweat. A few hours after eating, he spits his food up and chews it again for dinner.

Night falls, and soon it is time for bed.

The Camel Food Web

The food web shows how living things need each other for food. Camels mostly eat plants. They may eat fish or other dead animals if there are no plants. Their main **predators** are humans.

> **Predator:** *An animal that hunts other animals.*

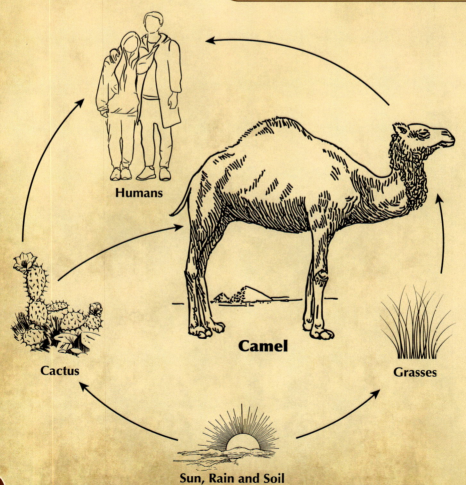

Humans

Camel

Cactus

Grasses

Sun, Rain and Soil

Dangers

Endangered: *In danger of dying out.*

Wild camels are **endangered**. People are taking over the land where wild camels live. People dig for oil on the land. People build on the land.

People let their own camels graze on the land. Then there isn't enough food for the wild camels.

Sometimes camels are hunted by people. Sometimes they are hunted by wolves.

Water Play

Camels store water in their bodies. They store water in their blood. They store water in their stomachs.

What can you use to store water? *Ask a grown-up if you can play with water to find out.*

It's stored in the sponge!

Put water into a clear measuring cup. Put a sponge in the water. *Is there less water in the measuring cup now?*

Get an ice tray or muffin tin. Fill it with things that might store water. *Does a cotton ball, paper towel or piece of paper store water? Do some things store more water than others?*

When water is stored, it can be saved to use later.

Glossary

Alpha male: The top male in a group.

Bellow: A roaring shout.

Caravan: A herd of camels.

Diurnal: Active during the day.

Domestic: Tame; not wild.

Endangered: In danger of dying out.

Feral: Gone wild after being tame.

Graze: Eat grass.

Herbivore: Plant eater.

Moisture: A small amount of water or other liquid.

Predator: An animal that hunts other animals.

Sweat: Moisture leaving your body through your skin.

Jokes and Rhymes

Llama was down in the dumps
Because he had no humps.
His cousin the camel
Was the only mammal
Who wasn't a hungry grump.

What did the camel eat when he crossed the desert?

Sand-wiches

Why do camels blend in so well with their surroundings?

They use camel-flage.

Riding a camel really isn't as hard as they say it is.

Once you get over the first hump, the rest is easy.

What is a camel's favorite day of the week?

Hump Day!

Why did the camel cross the road?

Because there are no chickens in the desert.

What's the difference between a one-humped camel and a two-humped camel?

One hump